19.93

Pebble® Bilingüe/Bilingual Plus

Dinosaurios y animales prehistóricos/Dinosaurs and Prehistoric Animals

Triceratops/Triceratops

por/by Helen Frost

Traducción/Translation: Dr. Martín Luis Guzmán Ferrer
Editor Consultor/Consulting Editor: Dra. Gail Saunders-Smith
Consultor/Consultant: Jack Horner, Curator of Paleontology
Museum of the Rockies
Bozeman, Montana

Capstone *press*®

Mankato, Minnesota

Pebble Plus is published by Capstone Press,
151 Good Counsel Drive, P.O. Box 669, Mankato, Minnesota 56002.
www.capstonepress.com

1 2 3 4 5 6 11 10 09 08 07 06

Library of Congress Cataloging-in-Publication Data
Frost, Helen, 1949–
  [Triceratops. Spanish & English]
  Triceratops/de Helen Frost = Triceratops/by Helen Frost.
  p. cm.—(Pebble Plus. Dinosaurios y animales prehistóricos = Pebble Plus. Dinosaurs and
prehistoric animals)
  Parallel text in English and Spanish.
  Includes index.
  ISBN-13: 978-0-7368-6687-3 (hardcover)
  ISBN-10: 0-7368-6687-6 (hardcover)
  1. Triceratops—Juvenile literature. I. Title. II. Series: Pebble Plus. Dinosaurios y animales prehistóricos.
QE862.O65F7818 2007
567.915'8—dc22   2005037479

Summary: Simple text and illustrations present triceratops, its body parts, and behavior—in both English
    and Spanish.

Editorial Credits
Martha E. H. Rustad, editor; Katy Kudela, bilingual editor; Eida del Risco, Spanish copy editor; Linda Clavel,
    set designer; Jon Hughes, illustrator; Wanda Winch, photo researcher; Scott Thoms, photo editor

Photo Credit
Unicorn Stock Photos/A. Gurmankin, 21

The author thanks the children's library staff at the Allen County Public Library in Fort Wayne, Indiana,
for research assistance.

Note to Parents and Teachers

The Dinosaurios y animales prehistóricos/Dinosaurs and Prehistoric Animals
set supports national science standards related to the evolution of life. This book
describes triceratops in both English and Spanish. The images support early readers in
understanding the text. The repetition of words and phrases helps early readers learn
new words. This book also introduces early readers to subject-specific vocabulary words,
which are defined in the Glossary section. Early readers may need assistance to read
some words and to use the Table of Contents, Glossary, Internet Sites, and Index sections
of the book.

Table of Contents

Tabla de contenidos

A Three-Horned Dinosaur

Triceratops was a dinosaur

with three horns on its face.

Triceratops had a heavy body

and a big head.

Un dinosaurio con tricornio

Los triceratops eran unos dinosaurios

con tres cuernos en la cara.

Los triceratops tenían el cuerpo

muy pesado y una enorme cabeza.

How Triceratops Looked

Triceratops was about
as long as a school bus.
It was about 30 feet
(9 meters) long.

Cómo eran los triceratops

Los triceratops eran tan largos
como un autobús escolar.
Medían cerca de 9 metros
(30 pies) de largo.

Triceratops had
two long horns
above its eyes.
It had one short horn
on its nose.

Los triceratops tenían dos
cuernos alargados encima
de los ojos y un cuerno
corto en la nariz.

A large frill fanned out

around the neck

of triceratops.

Los triceratops tenían una especie

de gola ancha y ondulada en forma

de abanico, alrededor del cuello.

Triceratops had four strong legs.
It walked across the plains.

Los triceratops tenían cuatro
patas fuertes. Podían atravesar
las planicies.

What Triceratops Did

Triceratops traveled
in herds. Herds moved
from place to place
looking for food.

Qué hacían los triceratops

Los triceratops se desplazaban
en manadas. Las manadas se
movían de un lado a otro
en busca de comida.

Triceratops cut plants
with its strong beak.
Triceratops chewed plants
with rows of flat teeth.

Los triceratops cortaban las plantas
con sus fuertes picos. Los triceratops
masticaban las plantas con sus hileras
de dientes planos.

The End of Triceratops

Triceratops died out

about 65 million years ago.

No one knows why they all died.

You can see triceratops fossils

in museums.

El fin de los triceratops

Los triceratops desaparecieron hace cerca

de 65 millones de años. Nadie sabe por

qué murieron todos. Se pueden ver fósiles

de triceratops en los museos.

Glossary

dinosaur—a large reptile that lived on land in prehistoric times

fossil—the remains or traces of an animal or a plant, preserved as rock

frill—a bony collar that fans out around an animal's neck

herd—a large group of animals

horn—a hard, bony growth on the heads of some animals

museum—a place where interesting objects of art, history, or science are shown

North America—the continent in the Western Hemisphere that includes the United States, Canada, Mexico, and Central America

prehistoric—very, very old; prehistoric means belonging to a time before history was written down.

Glosario

América del Norte—continente en el Hemisferio Occidental que incluye los Estados Unidos, Canadá, México y Centroamérica

el cuerno—protuberancia dura y huesuda en la cabeza de algunos animales

el dinosaurio—reptil grande de la prehistoria que vivía en tierra

el fósil—restos o vestigios de un animal o una planta que se conservan como piedras

la gola—cuello huesudo en forma de abanico alrededor del cuello de un animal

la manada—grupo grande de animales

el museo—lugar donde se exhiben objetos de arte, historia o ciencias

prehistórico—muy, muy viejo; prehistórico quiere decir perteneciente a una época antes de que hubiera historia escrita.

Internet Sites

FactHound offers a safe, fun way to find Internet sites related to this book. All of the sites on FactHound have been researched by our staff.

Here's how:

1. Visit *www.facthound.com*

2. Choose your grade level.

3. Type in this book ID **0736866876** for age-appropriate sites. You may also browse subjects by clicking on letters, or by clicking on pictures and words.

4. Click on the **Fetch It** button.

FactHound will fetch the best sites for you!

Index

Sitios de Internet

FactHound proporciona una manera divertida y segura de encontrar sitios de Internet relacionados con este libro. Nuestro personal ha investigado todos los sitios de FactHound. Es posible que los sitios no estén en español.

Se hace así:

1. Visita *www.facthound.com*

2. Elige tu grado escolar.

3. Introduce este código especial **0736866876** para ver sitios apropiados según tu edad, o usa una palabra relacionada con este libro para hacer una búsqueda general.

4. Haz clic en el botón **Fetch It**.

¡FactHound buscará los mejores sitios para ti!

Índice